Yo Mama So

Jokes So Funny Yo Mama Would Laugh Too

Published by Glowworm Press
7 Nuffield Way
Abingdon OX14 1RL
By Charlie Crapper

Yo Mama So Fat

These yo mama so fat jokes will have you laughing out loud. These yo mama so fat jokes are so funny yo mama would laugh too.

We hope you enjoy these yo mama so fat gags, which we can confidently say is the largest selection of yo mamma so fat jokes ever assembled in one place. Jam packed full of the very best kid friendly yo mamma so fat jokes; this book will have you in stitches.

FOREWORD

When I was asked to write a foreword to this book I was extremely flattered.

That is until I was told that I was the complete last resort by the author, Charlie Crapper, and that everyone else he had approached had said they just couldn't or wouldn't do it!

Charlie is a very funny guy, and is an expert at crafting clever puns and amusing gags and he is always pulling me up for some of the stupid things I say, but I think he is joking when he says I was the inspiration for him for this book.

Anyway, he will be glad you have bought this book, as he has an expensive lifestyle to maintain.

Two Ton Tanya

As you read through this ultimate collection of Yo Mama So Fat jokes −250 of them − try and pick out your favorite. It will be hard, as there are so many to choose from.

Enjoy!

Yo mama so fat when she jumped in the Pacific Ocean it became the Pacific desert.

Yo mama so fat her Polo shirt had a real horse on it.

Yo mama so fat she is a map on Call of Duty.

Yo mama so fat I ran out of gas trying to drive around her.

Yo mama so fat she gave Dracula diabetes.

Yo mama so fat when she twerks she becomes a wrecking ball.

Yo mama so fat she's on the seafood diet - she sees food and she eats it.

Yo mama so fat she's on both sides of the family.

Yo mama so fat she doesn't eat with a fork, she eats with a forklift.

Yo mama so fat all she wanted for Christmas is to see her feet.

Yo mama so fat the National Weather Service named each of her farts.

Yo mama so fat when she fell down the stairs, the stairs cracked up.

Yo mama so fat when she took a selfie, Instagram crashed.

Yo mama so fat she enjoys long romantic walks to the refrigerator.

Yo mama so fat she wears two watches, one for each time zone she's in.

Yo mama so fat her Apple Watch is an iPad on a rope.

Yo mama so fat she ate a whole Pizza....Hut.

Yo mama so fat she's "Large, Single, and ready to Pringle."

Yo mama so fat she influences the tides.

Yo mama so fat she just had a baby and said it was delicious.

Yo mama so fat she uses Google Earth to take a selfie.

Yo mama so fat when she sat on my iPad she made a flat screen TV.

Yo mama so fat her blood type is Nutella.

Yo mama so fat her only friend on Facebook is McDonald's.

Yo mama so fat she blocks the WiFi signal.

Yo mama so fat she laid on the beach and Greenpeace tried to push her back in the water.

Yo mama so fat her idea of dieting is deleting the cookies from the internet cache.

Yo mama so fat when someone called her fat she ate him.

Yo mama so fat the police use her as a road blocker.

Yo mama so fat she sets off car alarms when she walks by.

Yo mama so fat when she walks up the hill, people think the sun is rising.

Yo mama so fat she sat on Walmart and lowered the prices.

Yo mama so fat she went to a restaurant and got the group discount.

Yo mama so fat she sat on an iPhone and turned it into an iPad.

Yo mama so fat she curves space and time.

Yo mama so fat then when she fell from her bed she fell from both sides.

Yo mama so fat she was baptised in the ocean.

Yo mama so fat when her beeper goes off, people thought she was backing up.

Yo mama so fat people jog around her for exercise.

Yo mama so fat when she walked into her new house the first thing she saw was the basement.

Yo mama so fat they tie a rope around her shoulders and drag her through a tunnel when they want to clean it.

Yo mama so fat when she was born, she gave the hospital stretch marks.

Yo mama so fat she was born on the fourth, fifth, and sixth of June.

Yo mama so fat when she gets in an elevator, it has to go down.

Yo mama so fat her favorite basketball team is the Denver Nuggets.

Yo mama so fat she wears a sock on each toe.

Yo mama so fat when she went to the movies she sat next to everyone.

Yo mama so fat when she wears a yellow raincoat, people shout, "Taxi."

Yo mama so fat when the judge said, "Order in Court." she said, "Burger and fries please."

Yo mama so fat when she bungee jumps, she brings down the bridge too.

Yo mama so fat she almost turned gummy bears into an endangered species.

Yo mama so fat she did a belly flop and two weeks later they found water on the moon.

Yo mama so fat if she was a dinosaur, her name would be Jell-Osaurus Rex.

Yo mama so fat she puts on her lipstick with a paint-roller.

Yo mama so fat NASA thought she caused a solar eclipse.

Yo mama so fat I could travel halfway across the world and still see her shadow.

Yo mama so fat if she was bricks she'd be a housing project.

Yo mama so fat she ain't got cellulite she got celluheavy.

Yo mama so fat she needs a steamroller to iron her clothes.

Yo mama so fat when I tried to take a picture of her, I had to get a mile away.

Yo mama so fat she's got more chins than a Hong Kong phonebook.

Yo mama so fat the only time she saw 90210 is when she stepped on a scale.

Yo mama so fat even penguins are jealous of the way she waddles.

Yo mama so fat when she drives a car, people shout, "Hey it's the fat and the furious."

Yo mama so fat she blew out both her tires on her roller skates.

Yo mama so fat she don't skinny dip, she chunky dunks.

Yo mama so fat her neck looks like a pack of hot dogs.

Yo mama so fat when she got into the ocean Thailand declared a tsunami warning.

Yo mama so fat when she stepped on a scale, it read "One at a time, please."

Yo mama so fat when God said let there be light, he asked her to move out of the way.

Yo mama so fat even Bill Gates couldn't pay for her liposuction.

Yo mama so fat she has a KFC bucket in her hands at all times.

Yo mama so fat when she goes to an amusement park, people try to ride her.

Yo mama so fat her belly button doesn't have lint, it has sweaters.

Yo mama so fat when she farted in the Gulf of Mexico it caused Hurricane Katrina.

Yo mama so fat she broke her leg and gravy poured out.

Yo mama so fat when she went skydiving, people thought she was a hot air balloon.

Yo mama so fat when she lies on the beach no one else gets sun.

Yo mama so fat when she bends over, helicopters think her butt's a landing pad.

Yo mama so fat she goes to KFC and licks other peoples fingers.

Yo mama so fat every time she walks in high heels, she strikes oil.

Yo mama so fat when she went swimming, the Japanese harpooned her and took her back to Japan to sell her blubber.

Yo mama so fat they have to grease the bath tub to get her out.

Yo mama so fat it took Usain Bolt two years to run around her.

Yo mama so fat she uses a stick of butter for chapstick.

Yo mama so fat she woke up on all four sides of the bed.

Yo mama so fat she's got an eating disorder. She eats dis order, and dat order, and everybody else's order too.

Yo mama so fat they use the elastic in her underwear for bungee jumping.

Yo mama so fat I tried to hang a picture of her on my wall, and my wall fell over.

Yo mama so fat she shops at the Gap and now it's the Filled.

Yo mama so fat she has more crack than Whitney and Bobby.

Yo mama so fat she eats noodles with a forklift.

Yo mama so fat she sweats more than a dog in a Korean restaurant.

Yo mama so fat when she backs up she beeps.

Yo mama so fat she has to buy two airline tickets.

Yo mama so fat she puts mayonnaise on her diet pills.

Yo mama so fat her favorite word is gravy because she puts it on everything.

Yo mama so fat she shops for her clothes in the maternity section.

Yo mama so fat she was talking on her telephone and it got lost in her ear.

Yo mama so fat she has to pull her pants down to get into her pockets.

Yo mama so fat she thinks she's in shape, because circle is a shape.

Yo mama so fat the equator is smaller than her waist line.

Yo mama so fat when she lies on the bed she flops out over all four sides.

Yo mama so fat when she goes camping the bears hide their food.

Yo mama so fat one side of her lives in a parallel universe.

Yo mama so fat when she farts they have to put it on the weather channel.

Yo mama so fat when I pictured her in my head, she broke my neck.

Yo mama so fat she has to wear a spandex wedding ring.

Yo mama so fat when she went swimming Japanese whalers on the other side of the ocean harpooned her.

Yo mama so fat NASA classified her as a planet.

Yo mama so fat she makes Sumo wrestlers look anorexic.

Yo mama so fat when she goes to KFC she says, "Can I get the bucket on the roof?"

Yo mama so fat trains stop to let her pass.

Yo mama so fat when she was in school she sat by everybody.

Yo mama so fat the only liquor she knows is liquorice.

Yo mama so fat her part time job is being a tug boat.

Yo mama so fat when she jumped in the Pacific Ocean a tsunami wiped out half of Japan.

Yo mama so fat when she went to the movies everybody yelled, "Look King-Kong in 3-D."

Yo mama so fat when she runs everyone shouts, "Earthquake."

Yo mama so fat she has to eat with a fork lift truck.

Yo mama so fat I walked around her and got lost.

Yo mama so fat she has more rolls than a bakery.

Yo mama so fat when she went to the zoo she got put in with the hippos.

Yo mama so fat she has a gravitational pull.

Yo mama so fat she went to KFC to get a bucket of chicken they asked her what size and she said the one on the roof.

Ok, that's halfway through now - we hope you're enjoying this book.

It might be a good idea to have a breather from all these jokes - there are just too many to take in one go.

It can be hard when there are some many great jokes, but do remember to decide which your favorite is.

Ready? OK let's get onto the second half – another 125 jokes to come!

Yo mama so fat her stretch marks got stretch marks.

Yo mama so fat all dark matter from space is falling into her right now.

Yo mama so fat she has to fly cargo class.

Yo mama so fat when she had fever it caused global warming.

Yo mama so fat she thought the first 3 letters of the alphabet was KFC.

Yo mama so fat even God couldn't raise her spirit.

Yo mama so fat her feet need license plates.

Yo mama so fat she brought a spoon to the Superbowl.

Yo mama so fat she wears the equator for a belt just to hold up her pants.

Yo mama so fat her nickname is Fatty McButterpants.

Yo mama so fat when she sat on the rocket the rocket couldn't lift off.

Yo mama so fat NASA uses her farts for rocket fuel.

Yo mama so fat she has double width swinging restaurant doors in her house.

Yo mama so fat she has pictures of food in her wallet.

Yo mama so fat when she went to "In 'n' Out" she couldn't get in or out.

Yo mama so fat when she leaves the beach everyone screams the coast is clear.

Yo mama so fat she got stuck in an armless chair.

Yo mama so fat she sat on two Sumo wrestlers and got arrested for double homicide.

Yo mama so fat a truck hit her and she asked who threw that stone.

Yo mama so fat she has a shape of a Pepsi - the shape of the can.

Yo mama so fat her favorite children's book is "Three Little Pigs in a Blanket."

Yo mama so fat when she walks across the aisle at the theatre everybody misses the movie.

Yo mama so fat if you tried to kick her butt you might never get your foot back.

Yo mama so fat if she go skydiving up in the Northeast there'd be 6 Great Lakes.

Yo mama so fat when she jumped in the ocean she said "Beat that Moses."

Yo mama so fat her high school photo was a double page spread.

Yo mama so fat she bent the space time continuum.

Yo mama so fat when she got in her car she says, "Dam kids, they popped my tires."

Yo mama so fat when she stepped on the scale Buzz Lightyear popped out and said, "To infinity and beyond."

Yo mama so fat when she went to the zoo the elephants were jealous.

Yo mama so fat when she's in her car and she sticks out her hand, the car will turn.

Yo mama so fat she walked into a tattoo parlor and the tattooist said, "Wooaahh. We don't do murals."

Yo mama so fat when she goes out to eat she looks at the menu and says okay.

Yo mama so fat when she gave birth to you it took them 7 days to find you.

Yo mama so fat not even a fork lift can pick her up.

Yo mama so fat when she fell off the roof people thought it was Santa Claus.

Yo mama so fat she went to the airport and asked for a ticket. And they gave her clearance to take off.

Yo mama so fat when I thought I heard music from her cellphone in her pocket she pulled out an ice cream truck instead.

Yo mama so fat she can't float, even in space.

Yo mama so fat her kidney stones are the size of boulders.

Yo mama so fat she jumped in the swimming pool and said "Where did all the water go?"

Yo mama so fat she has her own orbit.

Yo mama so fat she sneezes bacon grease.

Yo mama so fat she sat on the bus seat and the bus tilted over.

Yo mama so fat when sumo wrestlers landed on her, they flew off into space.

Yo mama so fat she broke her own branch on the family tree.

Yo mama so fat she created a black hole because she has attained infinite mass.

Yo mama so fat even her Myspace has no space.

Yo mama so fat even Bill Gates couldn't pay for her liposuction.

Yo mama so fat she broke the 256 block limit on Minecraft.

Yo mama so fat when she swam in the Mediterranean, even Italy couldn't kick her out.

Yo mama so fat during pregnancy she went to the hospital in a tow truck.

Yo mama so fat she uses the highway as a slip and slide.

Yo mama so fat when she dies she will break the stairway to heaven.

Yo mama so fat she makes fat people look skinny.

Yo mama so fat she went bungee jumping and broke the bridge.

Yo mama so fat the only time she lifts weights is when she gets out of bed.

Yo mama so fat when she was in outer space she had more gravitational pull than all the planets combined.

Yo mama so fat they will need a bulldozer to bury her.

Yo mama so fat when she had fish and chips she used her belly button as a salt cellar.

Yo mama so fat you can print out a picture of her and use it as a paperweight.

Yo mama so fat she has her own energy source.

Yo mama so fat when she walks down the street, she creates potholes.

Yo mama so fat the only letters in the alphabet she knows is KFC.

Yo mama so fat not even Jesus could lift her spirits.

Yo mama so fat her favorite actor is Kevin Bacon.

Yo mama so fat half of her ass was in a parallel universe.

Yo mama so fat when she plays Mortal Kombat, Sub Zero can't freeze her.

Yo mama so fat she tried out for the Indiana Jones movie and got the part as the rolling boulder.

Yo mama so fat when she dies, they will need to make a whole new cemetery.

Yo mama so fat she went to the elephant exhibit at the zoo and had a family reunion.

Yo mama so fat her idea of eating pork is eating the entire pig.

Yo mama so fat she went to space and never floated.

Yo mama so fat it takes a bed sheet to wipe her ass.

Yo mama so fat she got an ocean side house and said her pool was too small.

Yo mama so fat everyone keeps asking when the triplets are due.

Yo mama so fat she got her ears pierced with a harpoon while she was swimming.

Yo mama so fat she hopped in a monster truck and made it a low rider.

Yo mama so fat she can name every restaurant because they're all in her stomach.

Yo mama so fat I thought she worked at KFC, but in fact she was their best customer.

Yo mama so fat when she goes on an elevator, it turns into Hellevator.

Yo mama so fat at McDonalds she looked at the menu and said okay.

Yo mama so fat you need a GPS to walk around her.

Yo mama so fat when she sat on the side walk she got a parking ticket.

Yo mama so fat she eats a prize pig for breakfast.

Yo mama so fat scientists are worried she's helping the earth become a black hole.

Yo mama so fat her shirt size is XXXXXXXXXXXXXXXXXXL.

Yo mama so fat when she's thirsty she puts a straw in the ocean.

Yo mama so fat she doesn't need two others to make a crowd.

Yo mama so fat the tour guide in the aquarium said, "How did this whale get out?"

Yo mama so fat if you had a dollar for every pound she weighed you could pay down the national debt.

Yo mama so fat when she got into her minivan construction workers had to tape over size load on the back.

Yo mama so fat she has her own ozone layer.

Yo mama so fat she makes the whale in "Free Willy" look like a little goldfish.

Yo mama so fat when they took pictures of Earth it looked like Earth had a pimple.

Yo mama so fat she farted in the ocean and caused El Nino.

Yo mama so fat she calls the apple orchard a fruit salad.

Yo mama so fat people at the carnival said "How many tickets to ride that blimp?"

Yo mama so fat when she steps on Wolverine even he can't heal himself.

Yo mama so fat when she goes up a flight of stairs she leaves dents in them.

Yo mama so fat fast food stock prices go up and down based on her eating habits.

Yo mama so fat she fell down and rocked herself to sleep trying to get up.

Yo mama so fat when she's going on an airplane, she her ass has to pay for baggage fees.

Yo mama so fat when she stands on one end of the Earth the other end lifts up.

Yo mama so fat she needs two washing machines to clean her panties.

Yo mama so fat the elephants at the zoo thought they were related.

Yo mama so fat they call her belly the low rider.

Yo mama so fat scientists proved that the moon orbits her.

Yo mama so fat when we talk about mother earth we are referring to her.

Yo mama so fat when she went to Japan in a green bikini, everyone screamed, "Godzilla."

Yo mama so fat she went to the store and tried to go down one aisle and took up two.

Yo mama so fat when she bent down, the Grand Canyon got jealous.

Yo mama so fat she was Miley Cyrus's wrecking ball.

Yo mama so fat she uses a car wash to take a shower.

Yo mama so fat when she sat on Home Depot it became Home Deposit.

Yo mama so fat if she could bend over she could disprove the laws of physics.

Yo mama so fat when she fell and hit the Earth, it caused the Ice Age.

Yo mama so fat she went to her favorite restaurant by herself and asked for a table for two.

Yo mama so fat I asked her what her favorite animal was and she said the ones I can eat.

Yo mama so fat she uses the entire country of Mexico as a tanning bed.

Yo mama so fat she ordered leg of lamb as an appetizer.

Yo mama so fat she uses motorcycles as rollerblades.

Yo mama so fat a picture of her weighs more than I do.

Yo mama so fat she has Sara Lee on speed dial.

Yo mama so fat she has to take selfies in parts.

That's it.

There were some great jokes in there.

We really hope you enjoyed reading this Yo Mama So Fat Joke Book.

About The Author

Charlie Crapper has written a number of joke books and has been voted Most Promising Comedy Writer Of The Year by the International Jokers Guild.

If you enjoyed this book, you can search for my other books on Amazon, including Yo Mama So Ugly Jokes and Yo Mama So Dumb Jokes.

If you saw anything wrong in the book, or you have a gag you would like to see included in the next version of this book, please visit the glowwormpress.com website and send a message – every message does get read.

Also please leave a review on Amazon telling everyone what your favorite joke was - that would be great and much appreciated.

Have a great day!

Made in United States
Orlando, FL
07 December 2022

25729283R00032